DEADLY BITERS

PIRANHAS BITE!

BY JANEY LEVY

Gareth Stevens
PUBLISHING

Please visit our website, www.garethstevens.com. For a free color catalog of all our high-quality books, call toll free 1-800-542-2595 or fax 1-877-542-2596.

Library of Congress Cataloging-in-Publication Data

Names: Levy, Janey, author.
Title: Piranhas bite! / Janey Levy.
Description: New York : Gareth Stevens Publishing, [2021] | Series: Deadly biters! | Includes index.
Identifiers: LCCN 2019060177 | ISBN 9781538257845 (library binding) | ISBN 9781538257821 (paperback) | ISBN 9781538257838 (6 Pack) | ISBN 9781538257852 (ebook)
Subjects: LCSH: Piranhas--Juvenile literature.
Classification: LCC QL638.C5 L48 2021 | DDC 597/.48--dc23
LC record available at https://lccn.loc.gov/2019060177

First Edition

Published in 2021 by
Gareth Stevens Publishing
111 East 14th Street, Suite 349
New York, NY 10003

Copyright © 2021 Gareth Stevens Publishing

Designer: Reann Nye
Editor: Meta Manchester

Photo credits: Cover, p. 1 Maxwell.Roche/Shutterstock.com cover, pp. 1-24 (background) Reinhold Leitner/Shutterstock.com; p. 4 Fabian Schmiedlechner/EyeEm/Getty Images; p. 5 Denitsa Ivanova/EyeEm/Getty Images; p. 7 Tupungato/Shutterstock.com; p. 8 Eric Isselee/Shutterstock.com; p. 9 Volodymyr Burdiak/Shutterstock.com; p. 11 Daniel Rocal - PHOTOGRAPHY/Moment/Getty Images; p. 12 Jupiterimages/PHOTOS.com>> /Getty Images Plus/Getty Images; p. 13 The Jungle Explorer/Shutterstock.com; p. 15 Elizaveta Obukhova/Shutterstock.com; p. 17 Symonenko Viktoriia/Shutterstock.com; p. 18 ET1972/Shutterstock.com; p. 19 Hayati Kayhan/Shutterstock.com; p. 21 Tier Und Naturfotografie J und C Sohns/Photographer's Choice RF/Getty Images.

Printed in the United States of America

Some of the images in this book illustrate individuals who are models. The depictions do not imply actual situations or events.

CPSIA compliance information: Batch #CS20GS: For further information contact Gareth Stevens, New York, New York at 1-800-542-2595.

Find us on 🅕 📷

CONTENTS

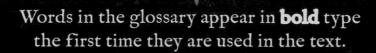

Words in the glossary appear in **bold** type
the first time they are used in the text.

In this book, you'll learn more about piranhas, how they live, and their sharp teeth.

CHEW ON THIS!

The word "piranha" means "tooth fish" in the language of the Tupí people of Brazil, a country in South America.

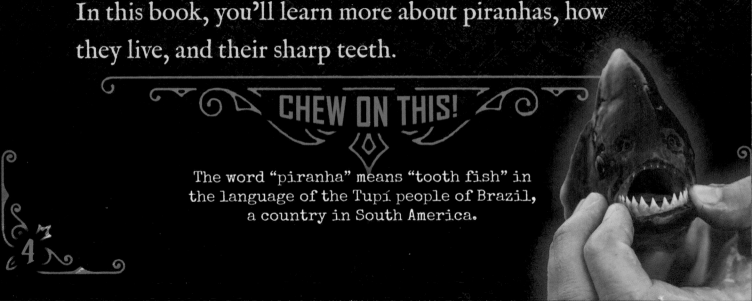

Over 60 species, or kinds, of piranhas exist.

HOME SWEET HOME

If you want to see piranhas in their natural **habitat**, you'll have to travel to South America. They live in bodies of water all the way from Argentina in the south to Colombia in the north. Piranhas are freshwater fish, so you won't ever find them in salt water.

You can find piranhas in rivers such as the Orinoco, the Paraguay, and the Paraná. But the best place to find them is the Amazon River. It's home to 20 different piranha species!

CHEW ON THIS!

Piranhas sometimes show up in bodies of water beyond South America. But these are believed to be pets that people have dumped because they can no longer care for them.

WHERE PIRANHAS LIVE

VENEZUELA

ORINOCO RIVER

COLOMBIA

AMAZON RIVER

SOUTH AMERICA

BRAZIL

PARAGUAY RIVER

PARANÁ RIVER

ARGENTINA

PIRANHA TERRITORY

Ancient piranhas appeared in South America
about 25 million years ago!

PIRANHA BODIES

So what do piranhas look like? They range in color from silvery with a red or orange belly, or stomach, to almost completely black. They may be as short as 6 inches (15 cm) or as long as 2 feet (61 cm).

Piranhas have a narrow body and a saw-edged belly that could be painful to touch. Their large, rounded head has strong **jaws** and thick, fleshy lips. Inside their mouths are some truly terrifying teeth, which are shaped like triangles.

Which piranha has the strongest jaws?
It's the red-bellied piranha!

BRINGING UP BABY

Like most fish, piranhas begin life as eggs. But before eggs are laid, males and females take part in a courtship display to draw in a partner. This display consists of the fish swimming in circles. That might not sound very interesting in the human world, but it works for piranhas!

After the courtship display, the female lays her eggs in a nest the male has dug. The male then **fertilizes** the eggs and guards them until they **hatch** in about 10 days.

CHEW ON THIS!

Piranhas can live 8 to 10 years.
That's about as long as the average goldfish.

Female piranhas lay thousands of eggs at a time.

TERRIBLE TEETH

Hidden behind the piranha's thick, fleshy lips are triangular teeth that are as sharp as knives. They're so sharp that people native to South America use them to make tools and **weapons**. And these teeth aren't scary just because they're sharp. Powerful jaw **muscles** give piranhas a strong bite.

Piranhas lose their teeth regularly and grow new ones. But unlike fish such as sharks, they don't lose just one tooth at a time. They lose all the teeth on one side of their upper or lower jaw. This means a piranha can be missing one-quarter of their teeth at one time!

CHEW ON THIS!

Even out of the water, piranhas can be dangerous. A single piranha can bite off a fisherman's toe!

Piranhas have just one row of teeth on both the top and the bottom of their mouths.

WHAT'S FOR DINNER?

Piranhas' reputation as terrifying predators might lead you to think they eat only meat and will attack any animal in the water—including people. However, that's far from true. In fact, an average piranha meal plan consists of bugs, fish, **crustaceans**, worms, **carrion**, seeds, and plant matter.

Piranhas also eat birds, snakes, and other small animals. They even eat fish scales, and some are vegetarians and only eat plants! Attacks on people or large animals are highly unusual.

CHEW ON THIS!

Sometimes, when there's not a lot of food to eat, piranhas will start eating each other. That means they're cannibals!

Adult piranhas look for food mainly in
the early morning and evening.

THE PETRIFYING RED-BELLIED PIRANHA

Red-bellied piranhas are perhaps the scariest kind. They live and hunt in groups of 20 to 30. When they're hunting, they spread out over an area. They hide among plants, waiting for **prey**. When prey is spotted, everyone rushes in. If there is blood in the water, the piranhas get more forceful.

The piranhas eat their prey in a very orderly way. Each piranha takes a bite and then swims away so another fish can move in.

CHEW ON THIS!

Several groups of red-bellied piranhas can come together in what is called a feeding frenzy if a large animal is attacked. This doesn't happen very often.

A red-bellied piranha eats about one-eighth
of its body mass each day.

SWIMMING IN SHOALS

The groups that piranhas live in are called shoals. You might think they swim in shoals because group hunting is the best way to hunt, much like wolves hunt in packs. But that's not true.

Piranhas swim in shoals because they're afraid. Lots of animals hunt them, including larger fish, river dolphins, jaguars, birds, and caimans, which are members of the alligator family. Swimming in shoals helps keep them safe from these predators. Older piranhas swim towards the middle of the shoal, and younger piranhas swim towards the outside.

CHEW ON THIS!

Even people catch piranhas and eat them! The fish are said to be great **grilled** or in soup.

Scientists found that red-bellied piranhas breathe easier in large shoals and are calmer when faced with a pretend-predator attack.

THE NOT-SO-SCARY PIRANHA

Perhaps piranhas don't live up to the scary reputation they have. Yes, they have sharp teeth and powerful jaw muscles that give them a strong bite. And, yes, they swim in large groups, which might seem frightening.

But meat-eating piranhas hunt small animals. And some piranhas only eat plants! In the very unusual cases where piranhas eat a large animal, that animal is already dead or badly hurt. And piranhas *do not* hunt people! So do you think piranhas are scary now?

CHEW ON THIS!

Dr. Herbert R. Axelrod spent 25 years traveling and fishing throughout South America. He was never bitten by a piranha and never even heard of anyone who had been bitten.

Even if a piranha bites a person, chances are the piranha will only take one bite, usually on the person's foot.

prey: an animal that is hunted by other animals for food

reputation: the views that are held about something or someone

weapon: something used to fight an enemy

FOR MORE INFORMATION

BOOKS

Berendes, Mary. *Piranhas*. Mankato, MN: Child's World, 2015.

Gagne, Tammy. *Piranhas: Built for the Hunt*. North Mankato, MN: Capstone Press, 2016.

Statts, Leo. *Piranhas*. Minneapolis, MN: Launch!, 2019.

WEBSITES

Piranha
a-z-animals.com/animals/piranha/
Discover more about piranhas on this website.

Piranha Facts
www.activewild.com/piranha-facts/
Learn more about piranhas on this site, and find some photos along with a video of a piranha feeding frenzy!

Red-Bellied Piranha
kids.nationalgeographic.com/animals/fish/red-bellied-piranha/
Find out more about the most dangerous species of piranha.

INDEX